W9-CPD-339

3 9082 10197 3397

Mario Molina

by Cynthia Guidici

Raintree

Chicago, Illinois

© 2006 Raintree
Published by Raintree, a division of Reed Elsevier, Inc.
Chicago, Illinois
Customer Service: 888-363-4266
Visit our website at www.raintreelibrary.com

For information, address the publisher:
Raintree, 100 N. LaSalle, Suite 1200, Chicago, IL 60602

Printed and bound in China by South China Printing Company.
07 06 05
10 9 8 7 6 5 4 3 2 1

Library of Congress Cataloging-in-Publication Data:

Guidici, Cynthia.
  Mario Molina / Cynthia Guidici.
      p. cm. -- (Hispanic-American biographies)
  Includes bibliographical references and index.
  ISBN 1-4109-1296-5 (hc) -- ISBN 1-4109-1304-X (pbk.)
  1. Molina, Mario, 1943---Juvenile literature. 2. Chemists--Mexico--Biography--Juvenile literature. I. Title. II. Series.
  QD22.M665 G85
  540'.92--dc22

                           2004025317

Acknowledgments
The publisher would like to thank the following for permission to reproduce photographs:
p.4, Newscom/Brian Snyder/Reuters; pp.6, 27 University of California, Irvine; p.9 Corbis/Becky Luigart-Stayner; p.10 Getty Images/Time Life Pictures/Peter Stackpole; pp.12, 16, 36 Molina Family album; p.19 Corbis/Danny Lehman; p.21 Photo Edit/ Cindy Charles; p.23 UC Berkeley; p.30 Science Photo Library/Cristina Pedrazzini; p.34 Getty Images/Photodsisc green; pp.40, 59 Corbis/Brooks Kraft; p.42 The Nobel Foundation; p.43 AP Wide World Photo/Martina Huber; pp.44, 50, 57 Luisa Molina; p.48 Getty Images/Stan Honda/AFP; p.52 White House; pp.55 Corbis/Stephanie Maze.

Cover photograph: Donna Coveney/MIT News.

Special thanks to the Molina family for their help in the preparation of this book.

Some words are shown in bold, **like this**. You can find out what they mean by looking in the glossary.

Contents

Mario Molina is a chemist who made important discoveries about chemicals that harm Earth's atmosphere.

Introduction

In many professions, there is an award given to those who excel. You probably know about many of these top honors. Every actor wants to win an Oscar®. Every musician wants to get a Grammy®. For scientists, the top award, more important than any other, is the Nobel Prize. Scientists who win this prize know that their work is the best in their field. And they also know that their work has made a difference to people around the world.

In 1995, Mario Molina, a **chemist** and professor at the Massachusetts Institute of Technology, received a phone call with good news: he was part of a team that had just been awarded the Nobel Prize for chemistry! Their **research** had changed the way we think about how people affect the earth.

Mario Molina is the first Mexican-born scientist to win the Nobel Prize for chemistry. He remembers how winning the Nobel Prize changed his life. "It was the most unexpected and exciting thing that ever happened to me," he says. "I had been living a quiet

This photograph shows Molina at work in his lab in 1974.

life teaching chemistry and doing research on the way chemicals affect the environment. Suddenly, my name was in newspapers and on television."

In fact, Molina's name had been in the news before. The research that earned him the Nobel Prize had taught people all over the world about a serious problem. Molina and his colleague, Dr. Sherwood Rowland, discovered that certain chemicals were harming the earth's atmosphere. These substances are called **chlorofluorocarbons**, or CFCs for short. CFCs are useful in everyday life, but they can also be very harmful.

You already know that plants and animals need sunlight to live, but did you know that too much sunlight is bad for us? Fortunately, high above the earth is a layer of gas called **ozone** that blocks the Suns's harmful rays from reaching us. Molina and his team realized that CFCs break down the ozone in the atmosphere, allowing more of the harmful sunlight to reach the earth.

In order to stop damaging the ozone, Molina realized we would have to stop using CFCs, but that wasn't such an easy thing to do. CFCs are used in many household objects. Air conditioners, refrigerators, and spray cans used CFCs. To stop using CFCs, we would have to come up with new ways to build the machines that use them. That would take time and money.

Molina and Rowland knew that getting people to make these changes would not be easy; their research called for changes in the way people do things. They knew that not everyone would want to hear the news they had to tell. At times, Molina felt frustrated by people who didn't believe that CFCs were harming the atmosphere.

Because Molina and Rowland struggled for years before their research was accepted, Molina was surprised when their work won the Nobel Prize. Still, he had known from childhood that he wanted to be a chemist. His studies had taken him to many places around the world. He was determined to do work that made a difference, and the Nobel Prize meant that he had achieved his goal.

What Is Chemistry?

Why does bread rise when it is baked? Why does soap form bubbles—at least for a few seconds? Why does sprinkling salt on an icy sidewalk make it safer to walk on? Chemistry answers these and many other questions. Chemistry is the science of substances. Chemists study what substances are made of and how they behave. They explore how substances **interact** with each other and what makes them change.

The science of chemistry began thousands of years ago when people wanted to find a way to turn metals into gold. Even though they were never able to create gold, their experiments taught them a lot about the different types of substances we have around us. This study of the substances in our world was the beginning of modern chemistry.

Chemists now know that substances are made of **molecules**. A molecule is the smallest part of a substance that has all of the characteristics of that substance. Chemists study how molecules act and react.

All kinds of scientists need to understand chemistry. Chemistry is part of our daily lives as well. The next time you take a bite of an apple, think about it from a chemist's point of view. What changes had to occur, from seed to seedling, from white apple blossom to tangy fruit, so that you can eat that apple? What will happen to the apple when it gets to your stomach? If these questions interest you, maybe you should study chemistry!

Cooking food often involves chemistry. When you bake bread, the heat sparks a chemical change that releases carbon dioxide, which causes the dough to rise.

This is a photograph of Mexico City in the 1940s. Mario Molina lived there during his childhood and teenage years.

Chapter 1:
The Early Years

Mario José Molina was born in Mexico City on March 19, 1943 to Roberto Molina Pasquel and Leonor Henriquez de Molina. Mario's father practiced law and also taught law at a university. Both of his parents believed that education was important, and they supported Mario in his academic interests.

When Molina was a child, he went to elementary school in Mexico City, the capital of Mexico. During this time, he learned to play the violin, and thought briefly about a career as a musician. However, by the time he turned eleven, Mario had already fallen in love with science, and knew that he wanted to be a **research chemist**. A research chemist is a type of scientist who does experiments with substances called chemicals. Like many scientists, research chemists have to be very creative, and also need good problem-solving skills.

This is a photograph of Mario Molina as a young child.

Childhood Experiments

When he was a child, Mario had a little toy microscope and a chemistry set. With these he conducted experiments—always under his parents' guidance. "I did not play with explosions or anything dangerous. I didn't have any poisonous chemicals," he remembers. "You can do very safe experiments."

Molina recalls one experiment in particular. He placed a piece of lettuce in water and left it to rot for a few days. Then he put a few drops of the water under his little microscope and saw tiny life forms swimming in the drops. "Few experiences in life compare with that magic moment!" he remembers with excitement. "The rotten lettuce was **teeming** with life, and I was able to observe with my own eyes what those famous scientists had discovered so many years earlier. I have been hooked on science since that time." With the help of his microscope, Mario was able to see for himself that even something like water can hold many fascinating living things.

A Supportive Family

Molina was lucky to have a family that supported him. They knew that science was important to him, and allowed him to use a bathroom in their house and turn it into a chemistry lab. Not all parents would react well to having their bathroom taken over for science experiements, but Molina's parents did more than just put up with his love for science.

"My parents supported it. They were pleased," Molina says. His friends, on the other hand, "just tolerated it." They didn't understand his fascination with science. For them, science was just something they did at school and for homework. It certainly wasn't what they did for fun!

Molina also learned about science and how scientists do their work by reading biographies of great scientists. He had important **mentors** in his life, too. Several teachers encouraged his interest in science. In fact, his aunt, Esther Molina, was herself a chemist. After Molina understood the basics of chemistry, she helped him take on more difficult experiments, even challenging him to do college-level work. Molina was up for the challenge. He spent hours in his homemade chemistry lab, learning more and more about chemistry each day.

School in Switzerland

Molina's family had a tradition of sending their children to other countries to study for a few years. This way, they could learn another language, explore another culture, and continue their education among new friends. Molina traveled to Switzerland when he was just eleven years old. At that time, much of the important work in chemistry was happening in Germany. People in Switzerland speak German, and Molina's parents knew that being able to speak German would help him in his career.

Molina enjoyed the time he spent in Switzerland, but something was missing. He still had not found a group of friends who enjoyed science as much as he did. No one his age shared his feeling that "it was very thrilling to find out how nature works."

Molina returned to Mexico City for high school and graduated in 1960. He already knew that he wanted to be a research chemist, and he decided that the best way to do this was to start college right away.

This is a photograph of Mario Molina during high school.

Chapter 2:
Leaving Home in Pursuit of Science

Mario Molina began college in 1960 at the National Autonomous University of Mexico, called "UNAM" in Spanish, for short. He began working toward a degree in chemistry and found that a new world was opening up to him. For the first time, Molina was with a group of people who shared his love for science.

During these years, Molina learned what it takes to be a scientist: "First of all, you need curiosity. You want to find out how things work. You also need creativity–to want to find out new things, the things that are not discovered yet in nature. You have to have patience and you need to work hard. But perhaps most importantly, you have to enjoy what you do. Then you will do it very well."

The National Autonomous University of Mexico

Before Mario Molina studied in Germany or in the United States, he attended college and got his first degree in chemical engineering in Mexico City. Molina attended a well-known university called the Universidad Nacional Autónoma de México (National Autonomous University of Mexico). This university was founded a long time ago, back in 1551.

UNAM has grown a lot over the years. Today, over 425,000 students take courses in accounting, chemistry, law, music, and many other fields. It is the leading university in Mexico, and it was here that Mario Molina began building his successful career as a scientist and a researcher.

Working Toward an Advanced Degree

By 1965, Mario Molina was on his way to becoming a scientist. He completed his bachelor's degree that year, and already knew that he wanted to continue going to school so that he could one day get his Ph.D. in chemistry.

In order to get a Ph.D., a student has to spend many years studying one subject so that he or she can become an expert in that field. However, Molina knew that he was not yet prepared to handle the difficult classes that he needed to take in order to get

This is a photograph of the National Autonomous University of Mexico (UNAM).

his Ph.D. He needed more math classes, and he needed to study **physics**, the science of energy and interaction between objects. Molina also wanted to take more classes in physical chemistry. This branch of chemistry deals only with non-living things.

Molina decided to first take all of the classes he needed and then go on to get his Ph.D. He left Mexico and traveled to the University of Freiburg in Germany to study. He spent nearly two years exploring the ways that different kinds of molecules combine to form a new, larger molecule. Later in his career, this information would help him understand how gases interact in the atmosphere. Molina completed his degree at Freiburg in 1967.

Molina took time to consider his future and think about what kind of chemical research he wanted to study. During this time, he took a few months off and stayed in Paris. There, he kept up his math studies and made many friends. Together, they discussed all kinds of important ideas in the arts, in politics, and in science. Having taken this short rest, Molina was ready to continue his studies in chemistry.

After his adventures in Paris, Molina moved back home to Mexico City. By this time, he understood what kind of classes a young chemist must take. He also worked for a short time as assistant professor at UNAM, where he had once been a student.

However, Molina was not interested in staying at UNAM, so he left Mexico in 1968 for the University of California at Berkeley. Berkeley is the oldest of the colleges in the University of California system. Ever since the 1930s, it has had strong programs in areas such as physics and chemistry, and many important discoveries have been made there. Molina knew he wanted to work with other scientists who were as excited about chemistry as he was.

Sather Gate is a landmark on the University of California at Berkeley campus.

Studies at Berkeley

Always ready to learn more, Molina took courses in physics, math, and chemistry during his first year at Berkeley. After completing his first year, Molina took an important step in his career; he joined a research lab headed by a scientist named Dr. George Pimentel. A research lab is a place where a group of scientists work together to study one topic in great depth. They do experiments that can sometimes last for years in order to learn more about our world and the way things work. Many important discoveries have taken place in research labs.

George Pimentel, Teacher and Mentor

George C. Pimentel grew up in Los Angeles, California. He worked his way through college at the University of California at Los Angeles, and got a degree in chemistry in 1943. Pimentel then went to Berkeley to work on the Manhattan Project, the secret government program that built the first atomic bomb during World War II. He was not sure if he wanted to be part of building a bomb, so Pimentel left the project to join the Navy. He worked on a submarine until the war ended.

In 1946, Pimentel returned to Berkeley to study chemistry, and he got his Ph.D. in 1949. He stayed at Berkeley as a professor and researcher until his death, in 1989. Pimentel was energetic and curious, and made important discoveries in several fields of science. He invented a way to study how molecules are built and what holds them together. He developed lasers for studying chemical reactions and energy.

When he was 45 years old, Pimentel applied to NASA's astronaut program. Out of 1,000 candidates, Pimentel was NASA's first choice. Sadly, an eye problem kept him from entering the program.

Pimentel loved to teach and write about chemistry. He encouraged high school and college students to become scientists. One of the many scientists who worked with and learned from Dr. Pimentel was Mario Molina. Molina remembers, "He was an excellent teacher and a wonderful mentor; his warmth, enthusiasm, and encouragement provided me with inspiration to **pursue** important scientific questions."

George Pimentel had an important influence on Molina.

In the lab, Molina worked with **high-power chemical lasers**, tools that Dr. Pimentel had developed. These lasers help scientists study what happens to chemicals when light touches them. To use the lasers, Molina learned to use other interesting tools, such as vacuum lines, which remove air from closed spaces. He also studied special tools that can "see" heat. Using these and other tools, Molina completed his first scientific research.

Molina studied at Berkeley during exciting times. Students and professors were thinking hard and arguing loudly about many important events, such as the Vietnam War. It was also a time when Molina had to consider how science can be used. Often it solves problems and teaches wonderful new ideas. But sometimes, it is used to do harm. "I remember that I was **dismayed** by the fact that high-power chemical lasers were being developed elsewhere as weapons," says Molina. "I wanted to be involved with research that was useful to society, but not for potentially harmful purposes."

Molina completed his Ph.D. in 1972, and stayed at Berkeley for another year to do more research. Just around the corner was 1973, a year that would shape Molina's life in important and wonderful ways.

Chapter 3:
The Ozone Problem

In 1973, Molina left Berkeley to join a new research team at the University of California at Irvine. This new job started him on a path that would one day lead to the Nobel Prize for chemistry.

Molina did not move to Irvine alone, however. While working in Dr. Pimentel's research lab, he had met another chemist named Luisa Tan. They fell in love and married in July of 1973. Since then, they have shared their research as **colleagues** and partners.

The lab at Irvine was directed by Dr. Sherwood Rowland, a chemist who had made important discoveries about radioactivity. All matter consists of atoms, which have a positively charged nucleus, around which negatively charged electrons move. Together, the positive and negative charges cause the atom to have a neutral charge. Atoms are generally stable, but some of them can suddenly change by releasing energy. This is called radioactivity.

Dr. Sherwood Rowland

Mario Molina knows that scientists must work together to solve difficult problems. He says, "One of the very rewarding aspects of my work has been the interaction with a superb group of colleagues and friends…" Of his many colleagues, one stands out: his mentor and friend Sherwood Rowland.

"Sherry" Rowland grew up in a family that enjoyed learning. "Our home was filled with books," he remembers, "and all of us were **avid** readers." In 1964, Dr. Rowland became the first director of the Department of Chemistry at the University of California at Irvine and helped start and build the program there.

In 1972, Dr. Rowland heard a lecture about CFCs in the atmosphere. This lecture changed Rowland's career. The next year, Mario Molina joined Dr. Rowland's research team to study CFCs. After just three months, the scientists knew that CFCs were not just an interesting topic—they were a threat to life on Earth.

Dr. Rowland has published more than 300 papers on chemistry. He studies how smog is produced and how acid rain affects plants. He explores chemicals that may be causing the planet to warm up. Rowland has received many awards, including the Nobel Prize.

Molina says that Dr. Rowland has been "a wonderful mentor and colleague. I cherish my years of association with him and my friendship with him."

Rowland and Molina at work in a lab at the University of California at Irvine in 1974.

Dr. Rowland gave Molina many possible topics to study, and Molina decided to study more about the chemistry of the atmosphere. The atmosphere is the mass of gases surrounding Earth. Molina was excited to learn about what happened to certain chemicals when they reached the atmosphere. In particular, he decided to study chlorofluorocarbons (CFCs), chemicals that were used in many everyday machines like refrigerators, air conditioners, and spray cans.

Over the years, a lot of CFC gases had accumulated in the atmosphere, and most people thought that they did not have an important effect on the environment. Molina wanted to see if this was true. He was excited to learn something new, but had no idea that his work would one day attract world-wide attention!

Experiments with CFCs

Rowland and Molina already knew how CFCs act when they are near the ground. They now wanted to know what happened to CFCs after they had made their way high into the atmosphere. CFCs are useful and easy to handle, and they were commonly used when Molina began to study them. CFCs are used in machines to cool things. They are also used in fertilizers and spray cans and to clean equipment. By the early 1970s, millions of tons of used CFCs were being dumped into the atmosphere every year.

Molina's first task was to find out what happens to CFCs in the lower part of the atmosphere. It turned out that CFCs don't change in the lower atmosphere. However, Molina and Rowland knew that CFCs eventually drifted into the upper part of the atmosphere. There, these chemicals have fewer layers of the atmosphere to protect them from the Sun's strongest rays. These rays are so strong that they break the CFCs apart.

What Are CFCs?

CFC is the abbreviation of chlorofluorocarbon. A CFC is a chemical compound, or mix, of chlorine, fluorine, and carbon. Thanks to the work of Mario Molina and others, we now know that CFCs harm the atmosphere. So why did people start using them?

The answer is simple: CFCs are very useful. They don't smell bad. They're not poisonous. They don't hurt other materials that they touch. They don't burn. They are gases that change quickly into liquids when they are cooled or squeezed. Their ability to cool down quickly makes them good at keeping things at a low temperature.

Before 1930, the chemicals used in refrigerators and air conditioners were poisonous chemicals that ate away at the metals they touched. And they smelled! So when people learned how to use CFCs, they were glad to have a new chemical that cooled things without any danger or bad smells.

CFCs were also useful in spray cans. As compressed gases, they created the pressure necessary to spray things like hairspray, paint, and deodorant out of a can.

Now that people know what happens to CFCs high in the atmosphere, CFCs have been banned from spray cans and are not used as often to keep things cool. A few CFCs can safely be made into tough plastic products. These plastics keep heat from passing from one part of a machine to another. Because they don't break down, they can't pollute the air.

Some common household objects, such as this aerosol can, release chemicals that harm our environment.

CFCs are molecules that are made up of three chemicals: chlorine, fluorine, and carbon. When the CFCs are hit by strong solar rays, they break into their parts. Molina soon saw that while the fluorine and carbon were not affecting the atmosphere, the chlorine was, and in a serious way. He had taken on the research out of simple curiosity. Now Molina and Dr. Rowland knew they were working on a serious problem that affects everybody on Earth.

The part of the atmosphere where CFCs begin to come apart is called the **ozonosphere**. In this layer of the atmosphere, there are many molecules of a gas called ozone. The ozone has a special job; it acts like a pair of sunglasses for the earth by only letting some of the rays reach Earth. It keeps most of the Sun's harmful rays from reaching Earth's surface. Without this protection, living things would be harmed or even killed by these rays.

When the CFCs break apart, the chlorine atoms have so much energy that they can destroy the protective ozone layer. Molina's research showed that just one molecule of chlorine can break up as many as 100,000 molecules of ozone! Molina realized that CFC pollution was a terrible threat to the ozone layer in the atmosphere. If people kept using CFCs, our protective layer of ozone would start to disappear.

The ozone layer acts like an umbrella, protecting Earth from harmful sun rays.

Molina and Rowland knew that they needed to share these findings. In 1974, they published their research in a scientific journal called *Nature*. A journal is a magazine where scientists write about their studies and what they have learned. The journal *Nature* reaches thousands of scientists around the world, so having their findings published in the journal meant that they were very important.

Still, it took a long time before people began to think about what Molina and Rowland had discovered and to do something about it. Since CFCs were such helpful chemicals on Earth's surface, people couldn't believe that they could be so destructive high up in the atmosphere.

In His Own Words

"I first just looked at the CFCs, and I didn't know that they were damaging the atmosphere. The first part of the research was just to find out what happens with compounds that are not natural."

"There is a myth that science is lonely work … but it need not be so in a college or university. Much of the pleasure in learning and discovery comes from discussing science with friends and teachers. The satisfaction of learning something new is amplified by sharing."

The Ozonosphere: Earth's Protective Blanket

The Sun makes life on Earth possible, but the Sun's rays also contain light that is dangerous to plants and animals. Fortunately, most of these solar rays never reach Earth's surface. A special layer high in the atmosphere protects us from these rays. This layer is called the ozonosphere. In this layer, there are many ozone molecules, which block the dangerous rays.

The ozonosphere is important but also delicate. Ozone is easily destroyed by chemicals that pollute the air, such as CFCs. Mario Molina's work has convinced many people to make sure that Earth's protective blanket will continue to do its job.

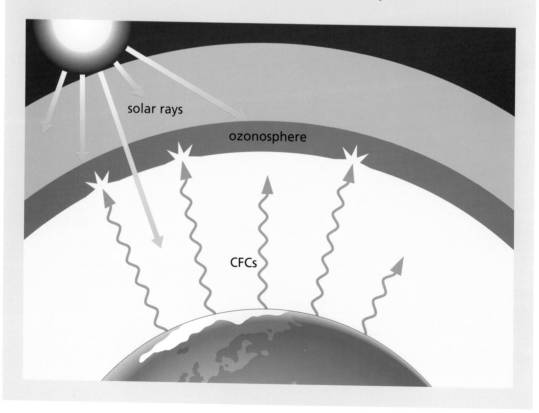

solar rays

ozonosphere

CFCs

This image depicts the hole in Earth's ozone layer.

This is a photograph of Molina with his wife Luisa and son Felipe in 1988.

Chapter 4:
A Man Who Does Not Give Up

After his research was published in *Nature*, Molina's life became very busy. In 1975, he began to teach at the University of California at Irvine. Then in 1977, he and Luisa had a son, who they named Felipe. All the while, Molina continued researching other chemicals that affect the atmosphere, and Luisa worked with him in the lab.

During this time, Molina and Dr. Rowland began to take their concerns about CFCs to the public and to governments all over the world. They spoke at many scientific meetings and published more of their research. In 1974, Molina and Rowland presented their **evidence** to members of the United States Congress. As a result, many governments around the world heard about the CFC problem. Soon, chemists began to work on finding gases that could replace CFCs and that would not harm the environment.

Reactions to His Research

Not everyone was convinced that CFCs caused so much damage to the environment. It wasn't going to be easy, or cheap, for people to give up these convenient chemicals. Even today, some nations still use CFCs because they cannot afford to make the change to new chemicals. And some people don't think that Molina and Rowland's research is correct. Still, Molina notes, "Practically all of the scientists who study the atmosphere agree" that CFCs damage the ozone layer. "Some people do not agree, and it's because they haven't looked at the evidence."

The evidence, meanwhile, was looking more serious. By 1982, after teaching for seven years, Molina left the University of California at Irvine. Although he loved teaching, he wanted to spend more time in the lab. He went to work at NASA's Jet Propulsion Laboratory (called JPL for short) in Pasadena, California, where he continued working with CFCs. In 1985, another scientist discovered that the ozonosphere over Antarctica changed during certain times of the year. During the winter the hole grew big. During the summer it became smaller. What was going on?

Ozone Changes at the South Pole

Molina, his wife Luisa, and their research group decided to find out. They set up experiments that copied the cold conditions at the

South Pole. Into these frozen mini-environments, they put ozone and then added chlorine atoms. The chlorine atoms destroyed the ozone, just as they do in the ozonosphere. But, under terribly cold conditions, the chlorine atoms break up ozone molecules more quickly and easily. This explained why a hole had been forming in the ozonosphere over the South Pole.

They were surprised to find that the CFCs didn't even have to float all the way up to the layer of ozone to damage it. Molina's research team also showed that other harmful chemicals were damaging the ozone in this part of the world.

Despite the new findings, people continued to argue about whether CFCs and other chemicals were really such a problem. People were afraid to give up CFCs because it would be expensive to switch to other chemicals. But slowly, nation by nation, the world began to decide that something had to be done.

Rowland and Molina began researching CFCs in 1973. They had to explain their findings many times to many people before people believed them. But they had patience, another quality that scientists need.

Molina and his wife celebrate news of the Nobel Prize award.

The Nobel Prize

In 1995, Molina's patience and hard work were rewarded. Molina, Dr. Rowland, and a Dutch scientist named Paul Crutzen received chemistry's highest honor, the Nobel Prize. This marked the first time that the prize was awarded for research on how people change Earth's environment. The debate over CFCs' effects on the environment was over. People might decide to ignore Molina's findings, but they could no longer debate whether they were true.

To win the Nobel Prize is the dream of scientists everywhere. It brought Molina great joy. Yet he understood that the prize didn't belong just to him. "I feel that this Nobel Prize represents a recognition for the excellent work that has been done by my colleagues and friends in the **atmospheric chemistry** community," he said.

In His Own Words

"I am heartened and humbled that I was able to do something that not only contributed to our understanding of atmospheric chemistry, but also had a profound impact on the global environment."

"We have to understand our environment, to find out if we are tampering with it."

"I have a lot of trust in the children, in young people. I think they are paying more and more attention to the problems of our planet. That's the big hope I have."

The Highest Honor

Alfred Bernhard Nobel was a Swedish chemist and inventor. When he died in 1896, he left his fortune to pay for yearly prizes for great achievements in science and the arts. Nobel, the inventor of dynamite and more powerful explosives, had great energy

to study, invent, and improve; he also wrote plays, stories, and poetry. One of Nobel's great dreams was global peace. The prizes given in his name honor people who do great things in the fields he loved.

Each year, the Nobel Prize is awarded to people who have done important work in physics, chemistry, physiology or medicine, literature, economics, and peace. In these fields, there is no higher honor than the Nobel Prize. Every year, about 1,000 names are presented to the Nobel committee for consideration in each of the six categories. Nobel Prize winners are people who are outstanding in their fields of study. Their work affects people all over the world.

A Nobel winner receives a gold medal, a certificate, and a large sum of money. Many scientists use this money to fund their research. When Mario Molina shared the Nobel Prize in chemistry, he gave $200,000 of the prize money to young scientists in countries that don't have much money for scientific research.

Nobel Prize winners Sherwood Rowland (left), Mario Molina (center), and Paul J. Crutzen speak at a press conference during the Nobel Prize ceremony.

Molina meets with students at his MIT office in 1990.

Chapter 5:
The Impact of His Work

More and more people were hearing about Molina and Rowland's research. By the late 1970s, several nations, including the United States, had banned the use of CFCs in spray cans. Still, it wasn't until 1987 that a worldwide effort to get rid of CFCs in the atmosphere was started.

In that year, the United Nations Environment Program held a meeting for people from many nations in the Canadian city of Montreal. At this meeting and those that followed, nations agreed that CFCs and other chemicals were dangerous and had to be banned. They created schedules for ending the use of CFCs. They also decided on **penalties** for nations that would not give up CFCs. Then they asked scientists from many nations to work together to find new chemicals to use instead of CFCs.

Today, there is bad news and good news about CFCs. The bad news is that not all CFCs have been banned yet, and a few nations have broken their promise to stop using them. The good news is that the amount of CFCs in the atmosphere is falling. And there is even better news: scientists believe that the ozone layer can repair itself. Ozone molecules are produced by sunlight, so new ozone is being made every day.

Still, scientists think it will take a long time before the ozone layer is as good as it was before CFCs damaged it. Some say the process will take about 30 years. Others think it may take as many as 100 years.

Teaching at MIT

In the meantime, there is still much to learn about the atmosphere and how people affect it. To continue his research in atmospheric chemistry, Molina left the JPL in 1989 and moved across the country to Massachusetts. He became a professor and researcher at the Massachusetts Institute of **Technology**. By 1995, his son Felipe was studying science in college, and Luisa began to work full-time in the research lab again.

During these years, Molina began to enjoy teaching. He was no longer in the lab all day long. Now, he divided his time between helping younger scientists in the lab and pursuing his own projects. Once a student who learned from professors, Molina was now a professor learning from his students. His group of colleagues had

Massachusetts Institute of Technology

Mario Molina taught and did much of his research at the Massachusetts Institute of Technology. MIT is one of the most important and well-known universities in the United States.

MIT's founder, William Barton Rogers, worked for many years to plan a school to train bright students in science and technology. MIT was ready to open in 1861, but in that year the Civil War began. Classes were postponed until after the war. Finally, in 1865, fifteen students began to study at the new school.

MIT's first classes were held in Boston. In 1916, the university was moved to Cambridge, and it began to grow. Soon, MIT became known all over the world for excellence in science and research.

Today, MIT is a world-class educational institution with 5 schools, 34 academic departments, and many different centers, laboratories, and programs. Students at MIT study engineering, science, economics, and many other fields. They work on research projects in MIT's labs and at its research centers. Students are fortunate to work with excellent teachers, including many Nobel Prize winners such as Mario Molina.

One of the newest buildings on the MIT campus was built by the famous architect Frank Gehry.

become larger. For Molina, teaching and research are activities that go hand in hand. Teaching requires Molina to think clearly and work through his ideas with his students, while research helps him continue to learn new things.

Molina's research continues. One mark of a successful research scientist is how often he or she publishes scientific articles, called "papers," for other scientists to read. Every paper competes against many others for the honor of being published. Molina's published papers show that he is constantly contributing new knowledge to his field and adding to what we know about the atmosphere. It's this continuous increase in knowledge and ideas that causes science to advance.

Molina's success and importance as a scientist is evident in the fact that he has published more than 50 papers. Winning the Nobel Prize was a high point in his career, but it wasn't his only goal. Molina knows that no matter how much he learns, something new and exciting is always just around the corner.

In His Own Words

"One [goal] is to work with my students and to help them become good scientists. Another difficult goal is to work with governments around the world to solve these big problems in the environment."

Molina works with students at his MIT lab in 1996.

Cleaning House

Molina's research has improved our world. By showing that CFCs harm the atmosphere and threaten living things, he has convinced entire nations to reduce the amount of CFCs that they use. But you don't have to be a chemist or any kind of scientist to help keep the earth's air and water clean. Here are three ways you can make a difference:

1. Recycle and reuse products whenever you can. Not only will you keep some trash out of **landfills**, but you will also conserve natural resources such as trees (used to make paper) and oil (used to make fuel and plastics).

2. Walk, bike, or take the bus or subway instead of asking someone to drive you. If you can stop taking a car to school or the park, do it! You'll use less fuel and lower the amount of gases that go into the air. And you'll get some exercise, too!

3. Plant something. Trees and bushes clean the air and put oxygen back into it. And they look great! When your city holds a special day for cleaning up and planting at the park or around the neighborhood, take part!

What other ways can you think of to "clean house" on our beautiful planet?

Molina speaks at the White House Roundtable on Climate Change meeting in 1997.

Chapter 6:
Science That Makes
a Difference

By now you have seen how Mario Molina has made and will continue to make a difference in our world by using science to solve problems. So you will not be surprised to learn that Molina continues to study chemicals in the atmosphere. Whether he is helping younger scientists, teaching at MIT, attending a conference, or carrying out his own research in the lab, Molina is looking for ways to use science to help the environment. He teaches his students that even the smallest changes to our environment affect the world as a whole.

Recently, Molina has been studying the problem of air pollution. He and other scientists at MIT and in Europe and Mexico have joined together to solve the problem of air pollution in large cities. They are studying Mexico City, where Molina was born, because it serves as a model for other cities. Molina knows firsthand how bad the pollution in Mexico City has become: "You can see it and smell it. The way you can tell is that you cannot see the mountains around the city."

Solving the Problem of Pollution

In 1999, a group of specialists in many different fields got together to fight air pollution all over the world. They started a program called the Integrated Program on Urban, Regional, and Global Air Pollution. Each person brought important ideas to the project. They realized that air pollution is a big problem, and the only way to find solutions is by having many people work together.

Some people, like Mario Molina, are chemists who understand how smog forms and how pollution can affect people who live in the city. Other scientists have studied in fields such as meteorology (how the weather affects pollution) and ecology (how pollution affects animals and plants). City planners and politicians who know how to put solutions in place also work for the program. And others are teachers who show their students ways to reduce pollution. Doctors also take part in the program by helping people deal with the health problems caused by pollution.

Molina's particular task in this program is to measure the levels of air pollution in the city. In 2002 and 2003, chemists used the latest tools available to measure various chemicals in Mexico

Mexico City is the most polluted city in the world. In this photograph, you can see the smog, a common sight in the city.

City's air. Scientists take measurements now so that they can compare the results with measurements taken in the future. That way, they can determine if air quality has improved.

If the many people involved in the Mexico City model project succeed, other large cities can use what is learned to clean up their own air, too.

"I feel most proud of having uncovered an important problem and that we figured out how to solve the problem for the benefit of people all over the world. It's the first example of a global environmental problem and the first example of a solution to such a problem!"

Encouraging the Next Generation of Scientists

Molina spends some of his time talking to young people about science and the environment. Many people should choose science as a career, he says, because so many problems still need to be understood and then solved. Molina is especially concerned about chemicals in the air that cause global warming and acid rain. He also worries that too many trees and other plants are being cut down to make room for new buildings. These plants clean the air and make oxygen, which people and animals need to survive. Water pollution is also a concern, since we must have clean water to drink and to water crops.

Sometimes young students ask Molina how they can become scientists. He has encouraging words of advice for anyone interested in science. First, he says, "Read about science and scientists." Stay curious, and "find friends who share your interests." And don't quit; it takes time, patience, and hard work to

Molina visits with students during a trip to Oaxaca, Mexico in 2003.

carry out research, but it's worth the effort. "But perhaps most importantly," he says, "you have to enjoy what you do. Then you will do it very well."

As for Mario Molina, he recently moved to California to teach at the University of California at San Diego. However, his research group continues its work at MIT, and he is still strongly connected to that university. He hopes to continue exploring chemistry today to help solve the problems of tomorrow.

Many Honors

Before Mario Molina received the Nobel Prize, he earned other awards and honors.

1983	Tyler Award
1987	Esselen Award of the American Chemical Society
1987	Newcomb-Cleveland Prize of the American Chemical Society
1989	NASA Medal for Exceptional Scientific Achievement
1990–1992	Pew Scholar on Conservation and the Environment
1995	Nobel Prize for Chemistry, shared with Sherwood Rowland and Paul Crutzen

In His Own Words

"Many Latino kids should become scientists because we need scientists all over the world from all different backgrounds. We have many tough problems to solve, and we need everybody's help to solve them."

"A good scientist can do a lot for the world," says Molina.

Glossary

atmospheric chemistry branch of chemistry that involves the atmosphere and how people's actions affect it

avid enthusiastic

chemist person who studies chemistry, the science of what substances are made of, how they behave, and how they interact with other substances

chlorofluorocarbon (CFC) chemical compound made of chlorine, fluorine, and carbon; it is useful in industry but harmful to the atmosphere

colleague person who works closely with another professional

dismayed disappointed

evidence proof; the reasons for believing something is true

high-power chemical lasers tools used to study the reactions of chemicals and light

interact to affect or influence one another

landfill system of trash and garbage disposal in which the waste is buried between layers of the earth

mentor wise and trusted advisor

molecule smallest part of a substance that has all of the characteristics of that substance

ozone gas that absorbs harmful rays in sunlight in the upper atmosphere, preventing them from reaching the earth's surface; it is also a pollutant and harmful irritant near the earth's surface

ozonosphere layer of the atmosphere that stops solar rays from reaching the earth

penalty sum of money or other type of compensation to punish a person or country for not complying with the terms of an agreement

physics science that deals with the facts about matter and energy; physicists study light, heat, sound, and the atom

pursue to take actions to obtain or accomplish something

research studies and experiments that lead to new knowledge, or the discovery of new information

research chemist type of chemist who does experiments in laboratories

technology use of science to solve problems in fields such as medicine, industry, or engineering

teeming filled to the point of overflowing

Timeline

1943   Mario José Molina is born in Mexico City on March 19.

1954   Travels to Switzerland to attend school and learn German.

1965   Graduates from the National Autonomous University of Mexico with a degree in chemical engineering.

1967   Receives a master's degree in chemistry from the University of Freiburg in Germany.

1968   Immigrates to the United States; enrolls at the University of California at Berkeley; joins George Pimentel's research team.

1972   Completes doctorate in chemistry from UC Berkeley.

1973   Marries fellow chemist Luisa Tan.

1974   Molina and Rowland publish their early findings in the important science journal *Nature*.

1975   Becomes assistant professor of chemistry at the University of California at Irvine.

1977   Molinas's son Felipe is born.

1979   Promoted to associate professor at UC Irvine.

1982   Joins the technical staff at the Jet Propulsion Laboratory (JPL) at the California Institute of Technology.

1984   Becomes senior research scientist at JPL.

1987   Molina's research is used at the United Nations to support the ban on CFCs.

1989   Becomes a professor at MIT.

1995   Shares the Nobel Prize in Chemistry with Sherwood Rowland and Paul Crutzen.

1996–present Continues his research in atmospheric chemistry.

Further Information

Further Reading

Chapman, Matthew, and Rob Bowden. *Air Pollution: Our Impact on the Planet*. New York: Raintree/Steck Vaughn, 2002.

Hauser, Jill Frankel, and Michael Kline. *Super Science Concoctions: 50 Mystery Mixtures for Fabulous Fun*. Williamson, 1996.

Hunter, Rebecca M. *Pollution and Conservation*. Chicago: Raintree, 2001

Kent, Deborah, and Michael Burgan. *Mario Molina: Chemist and Nobel Prize Winner*. Chanhassen, MN: Proud Heritage: The Hispanic Library. Child's World, 2004.

Newmark, Ann. *Chemistry*. New York: Dorling Kindersley Publishing, Inc., 2000.

St. John, Jetty. *Hispanic Scientists*. Bloomington, MN: Capstone Press, Inc., 1996.

Addresses

Massachusetts Institute of Technology (MIT)
Center for Global Change Science
MIT 54-1312
77 Massachusetts Ave.
Cambridge, MA 02139

National Recycling Coalition
1325 G Street NW
Suite 1025
Washington, DC 20005

Index